Contents

Senses

We all have five senses.

The Five Senses

Hearing

Rebecca Rissman

www.raintreepublishers.co.uk
Visit our website to find out more information about Raintree books.

To order:

☎ Phone 0845 6044371

🖨 Fax +44 (0) 1865 312263

💻 Email myorders@raintreepublishers.co.uk

Customers from outside the UK please telephone +44 1865 312262

Raintree is an imprint of Capstone Global Library Limited, a company incorporated in England and Wales having its registered office at 7 Pilgrim Street, London EC4V 6LB – Registered company number: 6695582

Edited by Rebecca Rissman and Catherine Veitch
Designed by Ryan Frieson and Kimberly R. Miracle
Original illustrations © Capstone Global Library
Illustrated by Tony Wilson (pp. 10, 22, 23)
Picture research by Tracy Cummins
Originated by Capstone Global Library
Printed in China by South China Printing Company Ltd

ISBN 978 0 431 19479 0 (hardback)
14 13 12 11 10
10 9 8 7 6 5 4 3 2 1

ISBN 978 0 431 19485 1 (paperback)
15 14 13 12 11
10 9 8 7 6 5 4 3 2 1

British Library Catloguing in Publication Data
Rissman, Rebecca
Hearing. - (The Five Senses)
612.8'5--dc22
A full catalogue record for this book is available from the British Library.

Acknowledgments
The author and publishers are grateful to the following for permission to reproduce copyright material: Age Fotostock pp. **9** (© Raymond Forbes), **18** (© George Doyle), **23 C** (© George Doyle); Alamy p. **5** (© Deco Images); AP Photo p. **20** (Al Behrman); Getty Images pp. **7** (Xavier Bonghi), **11** (Jupiter Images), **12** (Regine Mahaux), **16** (DreamPictures), **19** (Lise Metzger); istockphoto p. **13** (Plougmann); Photolibrary pp. **6** (Frederic Cirou), **21** (Pawel Libera), **23 B** (Pawel Libera); Shutterstock pp. **4** (© Maxim Slugin), **8** (© Ervin Monn), **14** (© Sonya Etchison), **15** (© Steve Mann), **17** (© Muellek), **19 inset** (© Jim Barber), **23 D** (© Maxim Slugin).

Cover photograph of a man whispering in a woman's ear reproduced with permission of Getty Images (David Malan). Back cover photograph of boys whispering reproduced with permission of Shutterstock (© Sonya Etchison).

The publishers would like to thank Nancy Harris, Yael Biederman, and Matt Siegel for their assistance in the preparation of this book.

Every effort has been made to contact copyright holders of any material reproduced in this book. Any omissions will be rectified in subsequent printings if notice is given to the publisher.

We use our senses every day.

Hearing and seeing are senses.

Tasting, smelling, and touching
are senses.

How do you hear?

ear

You use your ears to hear sound.

Your ears are on your head.

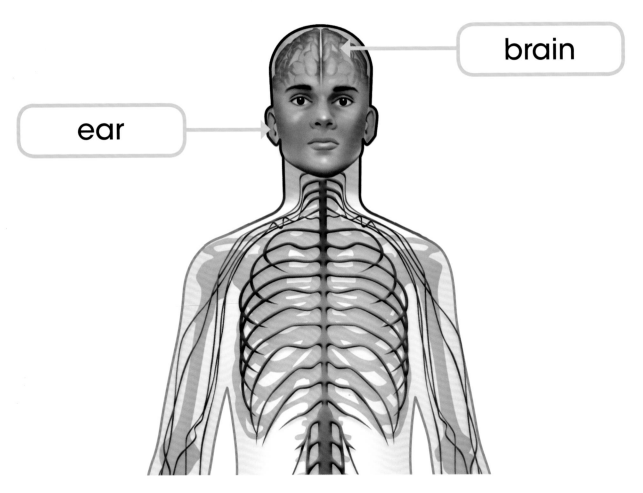

brain

ear

Your ears send messages to
your brain.

Your brain tells you what you
are hearing.

What can you hear?

Your ears can hear loud sounds.

Your ears can hear quiet sounds.

Your ears can hear sounds that are close.

Your ears can hear sounds that are far away.

Your ears can hear high sounds.

Your ears can hear low sounds.

Protecting your ears

Do not stand close to very
loud sounds.

Do not put things into your ears.

Helping people hear

Some people do not hear well.
They can read hand signs.

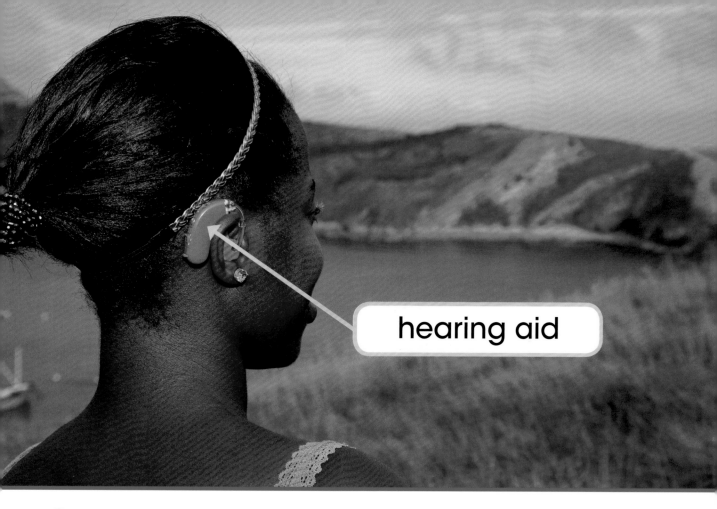

hearing aid

Some people need hearing aids to hear.

Naming the parts you use to hear

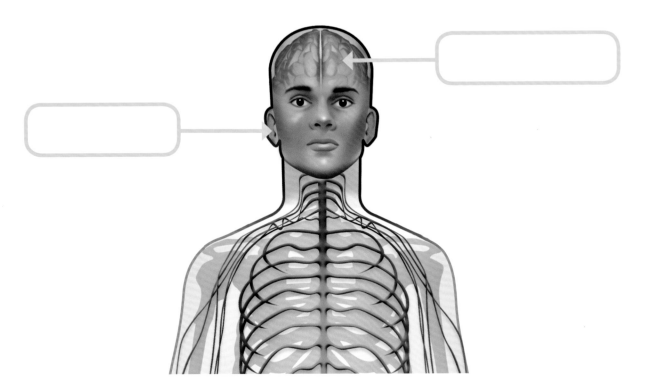

Point to where these labels should go.

brain   ear

Answer on page 10.

Picture glossary

brain part of your body that helps you think, remember, feel, and move
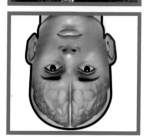

hearing aid small machine that helps people hear. Hearing aids fit inside and behind the ear.
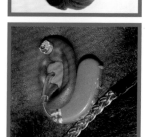

protect keep something or someone safe

sense something that helps you smell, see, touch, taste, or hear things around you

Index

Note to parents and teachers

Before reading

Explain to children that people use five senses to understand the world: seeing, hearing, tasting, touching, and smelling. Tell children that there are different body parts associated with each sense. Then ask children which body part they think they use to hear. Tell children that they use their ears to hear.

After reading

•Ask children why they think people have two ears. Have children form pairs, and have one child close her eyes. Then ask the partner to make quiet sounds outside one of her ears. Ask the children if they think that having two ears helps them to detect where sound comes from.

•Show children the diagram of the ear on page 22. Ask them to point to where the labels "ear" and "brain" should go.

•Ask the children to sit in a circle and place a selection of objects that make different sounds in the centre of the circle. Tell all the children except one to shut their eyes. Ask the child who can see to select one of the objects and make a sound with it. Can the other children guess the object?